# THE CLACKAMAS

## JANA HARRIS

The Smith

New York 1979

by arrangement with Horizon Press

ACKNOWLEDGMENTS:

Some of these poems previously appeared in The Nation,
Telephone, Beatitudes, Shocks Magazine, Passage, Plexus,
WPA 11, The East Bay Voice, the 1978-79 Napa College Cata-
logue, Off Our Backs, Anthology of the First Annual
Women's Poetry Festival of San Francisco, and the Sunday
San Francisco Examiner & Chronicle.

"The Men After Crossing the Gulf From Kodiak," ap-
peared in This House That Rocks With Every Truck On The
Road, Poems by Jana Harris (Jungle Garden Press, Fairfax,
CA, 1976).

"The Aleutians," "The Men After Crossing the Gulf From
Kodiak," The Skin Business," "We Fish Our Lives Out,"
"Memories of the Sally Foss," and "We Run All Night"
appeared as broadsides published by the Jungle Garden
Press, Fairfax, CA. 1976.

"I Canned Them Pears and I Canned Them Pears" appeared
in The Book of Common People, Poems in a dime store sack,
commissioned by The Alameda County Neighborhood Arts
Program, 1977-78.

design: Raphael Taliaferro
Library of Congress Catalog Number: 79-65679
ISBN: 0-912292-59-8

Women have an underground language, an idiomatic communication for cultural experience, because the real words are too embarrassing or unladylike. THE CLACKAMAS is an attempt to capture this language, to give poetic form and shape to the non—literature of female survival.

THE CLACKAMAS is Nietzchesque in the sense that it is an attempt in a reversal of values. Its intention is to exalt the trivial, the trivial as significant event. It is an effort to understand and explore the female source.

As Louise Bernikow has said, what we call literature is a history of choices. Those who have recorded literary history have not chosen to record the story of the women in the mill towns and fishing towns where I grew up. It is the stories of these women that interests me. My work is a resurrection of the "woman blues", a genre of literature that was heretofore not thought of as poetry and largely uncollected.

This type of writing, however, poses the following problems:

1. The literary tradition has been male writers creating female characters with lives and sexual lives as seen by men. Men have told us through literature how women are supposed to feel. When women write, we use these same male—created images, and they don't work for us. Therefore, female writers creating female voices is a break with literary tradition.

2. This is a patriarchal society. We are told that women's realm is trivial; gossipy, chatty, mundane. We are told that the events which are significant to women's lives are not significant events in literature. In creating literature we are taught to dismiss the trivial and, therefore, the day—to—day realm of women.

3. When women write about their lives, particularly
when they are sexually explicit, they run certain
risks; the risk of being called disgusting, the
risk of being rejected by men, by other women, by
academia, by the presses.

— Jana Harris

# contents

## THE CLACKAMAS

## ALASKA, LETTERS FROM THE PROMISE–LAND

## THROW 'EM ALL BACK

## I CANNED THEM PEARS AND I CANNED THEM PEARS

FOR Mary Kaczenski Brandon,
    Ron and Helen, Marj and
    Fred, Scott and Karen,
    and for Mark.

FOR their friendship, these poems.

# THE CLACKAMAS

## THE CLACKAMAS

White rocks
lined with cottonwood
and leaves the underside
like quarters chiming
in the pocket of my
borrowed—from—my—best—friend
summer dress.
Miles of river
lined in dead—car skeletons,
"Cross my palm"
says the gypsy lady sign
at the Carver Bridge
— Cross my heart, sweet river
shrunken by summers
almost gone.
I turn
find you
not beside me
like the buildings
of my childhood
torn down.

## MAMA WATER

They think they are the moon
these men
dragging us
mine to milltown.

Better company housing
up crick, they say
feed me, they say
bear me fish
buoy me up
fill up the empty holes, they say.

Eyes lit with the lure
of cabin cruisers and Cadillacs,
— money water
mama water —
once the sea filled over
the earth, they say.

And the moon a bit of child
thrown away.

# ALASKA,
# LETTERS FROM THE
# PROMISE—LAND

# THE ALEUTIANS

I read your old letters
the ones from Alaska
the ones from the boats
the purse seiners, the trawlers.
You say
you're waiting for crabbers
on their way back from Adak.
You talk about
getting on at the cannery
– it's King crab season,
boiler pots,
the two bad years.
Fish canneries
– PAN ALASKA –
factories using people up
like shoes.
You write
from a town out on the Aleutians
talking about the rubbish littered shacks,
the trailers,
your bunkhouse
when the roof blew off
and there were just the sides
covered
with playboy pin–ups,
men's magazines –
the smell of dirt,
smells of cigars
and women on the walls
advertised like "3 Musketeers"
to munch on
to fuck

to eat for breakfast.
It's the ambition,
the adventure you say
that drove you there,
living in the barracks
of an empty war naval station.
"Today, I walked on the beach,"
you wrote
"collecting seaweed,
the wind blows here
more than a hundred and thirty miles an hour,
the rain stings,
the ravens bark on the roadsides.
There are no trees on these islands
there are no women
there are no trees
and ravens bark
on the roadsides."

# THE SKIN BUSINESS

I went into the mountains,
he wrote:
Here the islands rise
6,000 feet from the sea.
I looked down, into the ice.
Down on Unalaska, Captains Bay,
down into the growl of diesel generators
and men shooting seals
near the trawlers.
Fur's big business here
pelts going for a hundred dollars.
And then there's that fox,
the Red Aleut Fox
with a thick hennaed tail.
I saw her up there,
chased her into the hills,
through the shale,
up to where the diesels are silent.
I got close, so close,
he wrote
I could hear scratching
on the crusted ice.
I chased her for hours
just to hear the claws,
Red, hey Red,
you ain't easy, Fox
you ain't easy.

But then there's seal hunting
- We could be commercial hunters,
you and I.
It's big money,
I picked-off five seals
just standing on the bow
of the OLAF AND JOHN.
And these hills,
these hills are full of Red,
I chased her over the glaciers...
We could be hunters
you and I.
Big money, each shot,
each spring of a trap.
We could get close, so close,
we could hear Red,
we could hear claws
running
on the crusted ice.

## THE MEN
## AFTER CROSSING THE GULF FROM KODIAK

From Ketchikan to Dutch Harbor
lusting the money of the northlands;
— Tanner Crab season,
the pipeline, the cold.
You say you baited Halibut hooks
crossing the gulf from Kodiak.
You say you feel good today,
telling me how it is
with the men up there;
men walking the front street
of Dutch Harbor.
There's this instant,
you say,
a category
made at a glance,
made like an insurance policy; like a dog,
"I got him
and I got him," you say,
"but Lee?
Lee's a big man in the company."
And then there's this Eskimo Tommy,
a skinny five—footer,
thick lenses and bad hearing
and homesick for Bethel;
calling the Philippinoes
at the cannery
half—breeds.
The men, flabby guts and fish—bowl eyes;
breathing tobacco alcohol.
Breathing the knives, the booze,
the words,
the drunken screaming

of a bunkhouse fight.
The men; you say
two men meeting
on the front street
of Dutch Harbor;
the glance,
"I got him and I got him,
but Lee,
Lee's a big man in the company.
Put me down hard.
So I watch." You say.
"I watch,
lookin' to change
the balance."

# WE FISH OUR LIVES OUT

On the boats all day
drinking.
Eight fishermen
and a galley table,
cups, half empty whiskey
tequila bottles,
cigarettes.
Talkin up big bucks
with the cannery women.
A couple of days ago
the skipper of the SEA SPRAY
fell overboard and drowned,
two years back
six men never got from the Elbow Room
to their bunks.
All look the same,
these beaches,
flat
the sea,
a desert
no one learns to swim in
and maybe just one body washes
ashore.
We don't just talk fishin,
we fish,
fish all the trips we've ever been on.
Fish the world, do decades of fishing
in a whiskey bottle
at the galley table.
We fish our lives out,
drink
crash
wake up
leave at 6, drink
fish till dark.

## GILLNETTER'S WIFE

He who stood by her, she said
like the mast whose shade
she sat under,
who would not take his knife
from the neck of the fish,
who cried at night
"Serena, Serena
the fish are like a ton of children
drowning on the deck."

Whose name he could not hear
her calling across the bow,
who would not take his knife
from the neck of the fish,
"Serena, it is like a thousand
of my little sons drowning."

Who could not hear her call
from inside the hull,
"the fish have your face
your face and my face,"
who would not take his knife
from the neck,
whose blood she could not
tell was not her blood.

"Serena
it is like a ton of children
drowning,"
who would not take his knife,
who was ashamed
because she would not use the blade,
who was ashamed
because she said
so that the others could hear,
"I will not stay and watch them die."

# MEMORIES OF THE SALLY FOSS

Wheel watch —
gray seas, ghosts,
volcanic islands in the fog,
and memories of the Sally Foss
that new shrimper
downed over west of Kodiak.

Fox Island
Rat Island
no lights at night,
only the williwaws
blowing the ice,
sweeping the islands
like a broom
into the Bering Sea.

At night
when the cones go off,
sparks
lava
holes through the fog.
Fishermen drunk'n wailing,
point to the ash
blown across the crab pots,
across the deck.

"Fox Island
Rat Island
black dust
bad omen,
no one live here."

# WE RUN ALL NIGHT

Left at midnight,
heavy weather.
The boat icing up, danger
big danger,
bobbing, maybe going under.
But we start fishing before the light.
Pulling pots
heavy wind,
crab pots
iron
600 lbs,
big as two telephone booths.
We pull em up
fulla Tanner crabs
giant crabs with macabre crab faces.
Rip em out
fast
breaking legs
pinchers
still thrusting
food
into their mouths.
We run all night
sleep at 3
fish again at 6
breakfast, fish till dark.
My arms ache
no money
— fifteen wounds
healing
in my hands.

## BENEDICTION
## FOR THE SALMON SPAWNING
## IN GRAY WOLF CREEK

they remember the creek of their foremothers
rise up
the steep cliffs
the rainforest
swimming against a glaciermelt
in Gray Wolf Creek
where I scrub camp pots
with wild moss
watching the salmon
down in their well

they remember the creek of their foremothers
rise up
looking like silver leaves
and sucker fish
a dynasty of daughters
resting in the dark
of a fallen log
like stones

they remember the creek of their foremothers
rise up
the rocks of this creek
are slick for you,
touching a broodmare's hump
I ask, is this it?
here with the thimbleberries
the cedar trees
the last stop
is this it?

they remember the creek of their foremothers
rise up
trudging on
past the trail's end
a bridge gone out
fish, we could make the decades by you
rise up the white water
rise up the rain
rise up

# THROW 'EM ALL BACK

# THROW 'EM ALL BACK

1.

He's dead, they said
filled this can with charcoal
trying to keep warm.
The camper
the state park at Vantage
dead.
Ya got the wrong guy, I said
that's some other body
an avalanche,
a boat wreck, maybe
when the dead—eye radar's
gone in the fog
but not quiet
not from charcoal briquettes
and trying to stay warm.

Or maybe he'll just call
sayin it's all a joke
that bright face knocking at the door
that schmerk
handing me an architecturally dried fish
sayin "here, Snail,
I brought you a little present.
It was a joke
a calculated emotional experience,
a transgression of taste
a little fun
now we'll go to North Beach
buy you a dress."
All those presents from Alaska
a taxidermied crab

an octopus beak
a joke.
It's a joke, I said.


2.

But they burnt you up
without me, didn't even write
the relatives
the names you couldn't remember.
Now I lay on my bed
with an empty list
of all the things I wouldn't do
to bring you back to me.
Your friends,
we spent a week
looking for what was left.
We needed a body
for the proof,
but all there is
is your empty truck
the cold wood stove
the hungry cat.
He's gone, I said
maybe at the tavern
I don't know
— running through the mustard fields
gone to play with my childhood pets
my guinea pig
my Pola dog.
Gone
gone to ash.

3.

Yeah, I said
I left him
so he couldn't leave me anymore
so he couldn't run off
to the lure of Alaska
to conquer the winds of atom bomb tests
and the ice,
so he couldn't hurt me.
        You couldn't
        anymore
        but even then
        you found a way.
        You did it up for keeps
        left me again
        the same pain
        bang
        bang
        you're dead, they said.
And this time
there's no salmon trawler
no seiner, nowhere on earth
I can send these letters to.


4.

His Ma says
he died of his own wrong life,
deserting the student loans
running out
drinking wine.
Says I left
made him so unhappy
that last Christmas of his life.
Yeah, I said

I was afraid,
spent a year on the couch
trying to figure it out.
Was it death, that energy
that light in his eye?
Was it me?
I could be dead, I said.
     But they forgot,
     those shrinks,
     they forgot to say
     that leaving you
     wouldn't kill the love
     wouldn't stop you
     wouldn't put the death light out.
I left, I said
that house, that smiling face
clear as a poppy
the day he went to swim
in the out—going tide
drunk on homebrew
came home shaking, almost drowned.
Left, left that smile
to haunt me
to light my dreams.
     Who, who was it
     that was gunnin for you?
     Who was it
     you were tryin to kill?


5.

     Was it your mother in me?
The relatives,
sad hags
had a good laugh on me.

But I got his face, I say,
his hand on my shoulder
the kick from behind,
since the day we met
I do the things I do
with his good wishes.
And if they try to steal
his house from me
I'll burn it down
I'll burn it
to the sound of his drunken laughter
I'll burn it
the way they burnt him
the way they burnt the only proof
I'll burn it down, I say.
    You know what crimes of passion
    are for.


6.

Dear Girl,
they write.
Received the photographs
you must have known
they would sadden us
people like you
bring out the worst
in this child's eye.
Wish you could have seen him
laying on deep red
edged with white
lilies
his last service
a blue shirt at his throat
his lovely auburn hair.

Dear Girl,
ask God to destroy the hate
help
to remember
to cherish
the love you once had.
It's the alcohol that's made all this —
for all of you
find ways to stop
the others
from turning
into ash.
Ask God for help.
Signed, lovingly
his cousin
his mother.


7.

We fought over you
when you were alive
and now that you're dead
we fight over your old auto parts
your skillsaws
your vacant lot out on the slough.
"Worth a thousand bucks
at least," they said.
But I gave em all away,
the tools
the electric drills
the one you zapped
through your thumb
on purpose,
the hole, you said
would release the blood

the pain
the hammer—smashed nail.
Gave em all away
to the friends
the girl you'd met last month,
gave em to that face that was my face
the braids
I'd cut last year
to Cassandra
whose letters were my letters
coming back
unopened,
hitching across the mountains
baggy Levis, goodwill boots
down to the orchard to meet you
to knock at your door —
he's dead, they said.
To my own nightmare,
I gave em all away.


8.

Dear husband,
I loved you and you left
so many damned times,
left me here
to face these brutes
the real estate agents
the finance companies
the relatives, the courts.
My dresser mirror is covered
with your photos
postcards of you
from Chelan, Unalaska, Michoacan.
And there's nowhere on earth

I can send these letters to
no fishing trawler
on the waves of grief
on the sea of the dead —
there are no tides
no telling when
the crash comes above my head.
We fished the seas out
you and I
the one the other
the rudder the sail.
How many, how many fish
have these hands caught?
To see your smile
and those calloused thumbs
the wounds healing
in your palms
to run them across my face
snag my cheek
one last time.
How many?
The urn, the ash
"Throw em to the four winds"
you said,
"throw em to the fish
the waves, shit baby
I don't care, God damn it"
you said.
"Throw em all back."

# FIVE EAGLES WATCHED

<u>Poem for Dead Husband</u>

1.

Me and you
we had it all
all the neurosis
German parents
obsessed
with poverty
and good taste
would allow.
The getting
the working three jobs
saving up years
like canned peaches.
On the road
moving through
a thousand miles
of goat hovel
shanties
and still—born dreams,
we had it all.


2.

Look—alikes
with our slanty—eyed
Hun mamas.
Me playin big sister
got ya to the dentist on time,
you played the daddy
helping me off the roof
patching shingles

the day
five eagles
watched
wordless
from a dead—topped spruce.


3.

I should write you
that the corn came up
in December,
write you
my last night's dream:
You in the kitchen
at a faculty party
cutting onions
on my pig board.
Me sayin
come back
please
come back
and you
— smiling face —
No, baby,
— laugh —
I ain't never
I ain't never
comin back.
I should write you that.


4.

What about the gossip
sayin ya done yourself in
— but I know.

I know the day you died
you did things
you'd never do.
You weren't there
alone,
somebody else
got you in that hole.
Trouble is
I don't know where to start,
some of em had you there
for thirty years
and some
some just hit on you
by accident.


5.

I write the news
over and over
— on November 9th
working near Lake Chelan...
he always spoke so well of you.
Over and over
a naughty school girl
given a hundred sentences
"I will not chew gum in class"
"I will not chew gum in class"
cause this would make me a better girl.
His friends sayin they're sorry
but no matter how many times
I write this letter
they'll never think
I'm good.

6.

That German heritage
blue eyes
and a young grave
I told you
I told everyone
and nobody listened.
So how come
it's just me
yellin <u>Murder</u>?
Those Germans
driving stakes
through the blond faces
of their children,
the wars
the wars
that killed you
before you were born.
The smell of guns
fallen logs
on a flat car
steel tracks
sliding knives
through the moon.
It's murder, I say,
cleaning my rifle
the one you used
to hunt deer, you said.
Your face
Hugo Blanco
your face is buried
all over Germany.
I'll get em, I say,
but how come
how come it's just me
yellin <u>murder</u>.

7.

Your name
your name
taught me
the hammer
the nail
catspaw pulling
cedar sliding
off the shed.
Your name
wailing
on the metal roof
— the one we stole
off the barn
by the slough.
Your name
your name
rolling at the end
of the tide
forever prevailing.
Listen.

## I CANNED THEM PEARS AND I CANNED THEM PEARS

## I CANNED THEM PEARS
## AND I CANNED THEM PEARS

I used to wait under that tree
she said, for him.
I canned them pears
and I canned them pears
cause he loved em
he loved that tree more'n anythin
— queen of fruits, he'd say.
I used to wait under that tree
for him, for the five o'clock whistle,
pickin pears.
And when he died
I didn't can em up no more
never did like em much
I give em to the neighbors
to my brother in Walla Walla
but he don't _do_ for himself
and then they fall on the ground
and rot
and comes all them bees.
I got tired
of waitin for the bees
to settle down
and tired of gettin stung
seein them pears
rot and him not here
to eat em.
Now people tellin me they're sorry
my pear tree died
real sorry
ol' tree like that, they say
big wind come an' split it down the middle.
Tellin me they're sorry

cause them trees
leave such terrible scars
when the bulldozer come to pull em out.
I tied baling wire 'round the trunk, she said
that fall after he died,
and it took two maybe three years
for that tree to die
I killed it, she said
I killed it.
I canned them pears
and I canned them pears.

# DAHLIAS ON SAMISH ISLAND

Chartreuse moss
on the shake roof
the shed swollen shut
by rain.
Indoors
maroon feathered wallpaper
shouts—out the paint
and there is nothing to do
but watch the water
stand on the streets
for days
nothing to do
but watch the rain
mow the wheat
the sweetcorn
falling with the green hills
at the edge of the Sound.
Only the Dahlias
bright in the afternoon
lighting the bare board house
lined by south winds
and years of gillnetters
coming up the slough
without a catch.
Here, even the fish
are gone.

# NO

Commuting
to that job
that's gonna get me free
the last year
last month last mile
of asphalt utility poles
of people's coca-cola companies
people's nabisco
people's award winning low-income
high rises and
CHUCK DESTRUCT machines
smashing 1910 Victorians
for Harriet Tubman Condos

Driving a hundred miles
of stop lights
stalled-out semi trailers
blocking exit signs
blocking the woman with blood
coming out of her mouth

Thinking of you
my friend
dead at 32
thinking of you commuting
a life of concrete
and broken yellow lines
thinking
no one will give me back this day

# HIGH SCHOOL REUNION
# AT THE ELKS

My Clackamas Hi
senior pictures
— me and Sue Cora
sittin on the fire truck
with that English teacher
tellin us to say
<u>no</u>
for modesty's sake
and Alvin Dooley screamin
"Sue Cora's on the rag
I saw a kotex in her purse"
but then we gotta get off the truck
cause Sue Cora's yellin
that she'll bust his arm
if he don't shut—up
and that's not actin
lady—like and adult

And now she's probably
up at the Rocky Butte
re—hab facility
for bein untidy on the street
they say
and at the next table
some insurance guy I don't recognize
is tellin his wife:
You ever hear of North Beach?
she did it all on stage, he says
she did everythin
even busted her hymen
right in front of me, he says
and his wife giggles
sayin, Oh take me
oh take me there

## NORMA AT THE A&W DRIVE—IN

Me and Rhonda draggin the strip
goin to the A&W drive—in
to watch Rhonda's ex sister—in—law
Norma
rollerskate her big butt around
car to car.
We'd order a mamaburger
and bloody fingers "to go"
wipin the catsup and french fry grease
all over the tray
so Norma'd have to clean it up.
Sayin she was havin another kid
ruinin Rhonda's good family name.
Laughin, sayin she oughta call this one TARGET
cause every guy in Molalla'd
had a shot at it.
Talkin about Norma being four months pregnant
and Rhonda's Ma even asked her
if there was anythin she needed
to walk down the aisle.
But there goes Norma
with a giant run in her nylons —
and every one of Rhonda's family
was so embarrassed
they coulda died.

# YOU
## YOU WERE LIKE THE CLACKAMAS

You were like the Clackamas
where I swam my tight
salesgirl muscles
swan necked
to keep my Saturday night
hairdo
from gettin wet.
Even in August
that water kept the skin
under my ruffled
polka-dot bikini
cold and needle pricked.
You were like the Clackamas,
swimmin with the white water
when I went your way,
goin with the silver fish.
And those currents,
swimmin up-stream
would give me strong arms
you said.
Eatin the bank beneath me
in the night,
drownin my sweet-smellin porch vine
leavin me
another Red Cross flood victim
in milltown
strip-city motels.
And now that you're
not there
and that you're
never goin to be there,
you, you were like the Clackamas.

## AT CHOW'S CHINESE CHUCK WAGON

On Sundays
Ma'd take us out
to the all you can eat
Chinese chuck
— that family in the next booth
with a girl and a boy
sucking his finger
stroking a receiving blanket.
"Looks like it's been
through the shredder,"
my Ma said
as he kept tryin
to stick the strips
of synthetic satin trim
into his mouth.
And when his dad made his ma
hide it in a grocery sack
he screamed
"gi'me my <u>bubby</u> back,"
all through dinner
with his ma tellin
his little sister
to pull down her dress
and the dad sayin
he was gunna leave
til they got better.
Later, on my way
to the Mode—o—Day dress shop,
I saw them
standin out front of
the cycle store,
saw the dad rubbin the seat
of a shiney Bultaco
dirt bike,

touchin the on—off switch
in a particular way
holdin the plastic dial
with his thumb and forefinger,
not to start the motor
but like a clitoris
to fondle.

# ON THE RAG

She cut up the old diapers
into kleenex size strips
wore them pinned
to her white cotton underwear
and filled them with blood,
washed them,
hung them
on the clothesline
in the mustard field
where me and LeRoy
played
<u>kapow–kapow</u> <u>ya</u> <u>got</u> <u>me</u>
with old croquet stakes
that the people who'd lived there
before us had left.
And when LeRoy asks
how come ya got
all them ol' dishrags
— which he never did —
don't tell him
what those are for
Ma said.
Don't tell him
what those are for.

## PORTRAIT OF
## A GIRL AND HER HORSE, 1965

I think of you often,
my sorrel Goldico horse.
You, who were the red
of the ribbed evening sky.
Hot summer days
belly—heavy in foal
we rode past the men
at the rock quarry
unafraid
rode through the aphrodisiac fields
of new mown hay
watching the flight of eagles
tormented by crows.
Behind the arch of your neck
I rode
to the rocks of the Clackamas River
worshiping
the bronzed power of your thighs.
Chariot horse
you swam the white water,
carried me sand—bar to sand—bar
til we were numb.
And those currents that drove us
across the mossed—granite rocks,
you knew them well
though they were silent
you knew them like the eels know them
knew them
like you knew the paths of the sun.
Goldico
those were summers with nights
too thick for sleeping

I drowned the dark spots of my soul
in that river
drifting downstream.
But now
though I know where you graze
with another foal
on some far hill near Oregon City
I cannot touch
what has gone.

## ALASKA

She don't get bored up there
she says talkin
about walkin Main Street
alone at 3 a.m.
when he's out on the boats,
cause everybody knows
her old man
is one bad hombre.

Talkin about fightin
plywood contracts with the Japs,
fightin fish
with an Aleut
— those salmon
gill torn and dyin on the decks,
big as her girl
she says.

Says she's been
watchin the herring die out,
ya can taste it
they got this sick flavor now,
but up there,
says she don't think
about goin to bed and not
gettin up for a year.

Gotta be up
to watch for the boats,
she says,
gotta be there on Dry Bay Bridge
or else
those boats might not
come back, she says.

## CONVERSATION
## AT THE SQUIRREL CAGE SALOON

He was a terrific muff—diver, she said
but now there's my CETA job
at eight in the mornin
readin stories
to fourth graders.
Marla's got a very old face
for a fourth grader, she said.
Marla's emotionally disturbed
always wettin her pants in class
and everyone sayin she's fat
and smells like pee.
I read Marla stories
out in the hall, she said
while I think of him
the muff—diver.

## FIX ME A SALAMI SANDWICH
## HE SAID

Fix me a salami sandwich
he said
I don't wanna fix it myself
if you love me
you'll fix me a sandwich
you have to help me, he said
you have to take care of me
sometimes
he said
I need mothering
I need you to tell me
you love me
I need to hear you say it
I need you to sleep with me
I need you to fuck me
I need you to be on top
when we fuck
what time is it?
where's those phone numbers
that green matchbook with the raised
gold lettering
with the phone numbers
on the inside

I put it right here
I'm hungry
I haven't had time to get to the grocery
I need comforting
I need a ride to the corner
Let's have coffee together for once
he said
you make coffee
he said
I don't like these raw vegetables
I don't like this smelly cheese
it smells like cunt
he said
it smells like I have pussy
all over my fingers
you don't take care of me
he said
I have needs
he said
I have certain needs
and you don't do "Mommy"
very well, he said
you don't do "Mommy"
at all, he said.

## CALIFORNIA LIVING

Close the doors to the lanai
the floors'll get dirty, she says
pushing the buttons on her microwave oven
mixing drinks at the rococo bar.
But then she makes us leave
for an hour
cause it's gotta be like Christmas
in Sweden
with the smell of baked cabbage
all through the house.
We go out past the master bedroom
– uncurtained
an enormous bed
the one the army shipped back
with their Cadillac,
her hope chest covered
with socks and sewing thread
and his shirts and his slippers
all over the cold linoleum floor.
Oh don't look in there, she says
we just sleep there
I just store things nobody needs
there.

## GARAGE SALE

2 navy wives
and thirty years
of her mama's discards,
talkin about the clientele
that down—the—block woman
— if she comes back
gunna call the cops, they say
just an alcoholic
the old lady kind
havin to go home
for a nickel in change.
Talkin about WORKING MOTHERS
and their little seven—year—olds
gettin raped on the way to school:
Three of em got it just last week.
School called one ma
said she couldn't come down
til coffee break
said to tell her kid
"just go to class"
have the secretary
clean her up, she says
— what's wrong with them schools
anyway.
Hope my next stop
we live on base where it's safe,
none of this riff—raff
off—base housing for me
can't let my kid off the porch
people sayin I'm too protective
don't let her cross the street
playin with that divorcee's brat
down the block
ain't gunna let my girl get kidnapped.

You hear about that nine-year-old
on the news?
They gunna find her
dumped in the slough, they are.
Sellin all my mama's stuff, movin out,
50 Get Well cards for a dollar
these linens, honey?
and that cute apron with that girl
in a 3-d skirt and see-through panties
appliqued on the front...
They never caught him neither, the rapist
three little girls in a week
but one, she was twelve
so it weren't so bad for her
she knew what was goin on.

# AND SHE,
## SHE WAS ABOUT MY MOTHER'S AGE

I'm tired, I said
and she, she was about my mother's age.
But you haven't worked, she said
the men have been working since 5
on the boats
they want lunch,
with that Hun stare
that high cheek-boned grin.
I'm tired, I said
– remembering my Ma's hands'
stale smell
from washing dishes in rubber gloves –
I couldn't sleep
thinking about turning thirty
alone and broke, I said.
But the men have been working since 5, she,
she was about my mother's age
the arty type
hiding lifetime canvases
in the attic,
rinsing off paint brushes
with charm school chit chat
to save the oceans
and fix lunch
for the men.
– That smell,
like Ma's rubber gloves
and the gray concrete sink:
"Just look at your daughter," Ma'd said
"got her ugly face on
cause she's gotta do a dish."
(pointing me out to the men

as I scrubbed pots
one August noon
near my 15th birthday
in the tiny two room apartment
with a baggy kotex
and a sanitary napkin belt
under my too big
handmedown bermudas,
tellin me I'd forget the bad
and remember the good) —
I'm tired, I said.

# TO RECORD THIS DAY

<u>August</u>   <u>Skagit Bay, Washington</u>

To record this day —

she sits
on the bare board stoop
under the apple
blooming even in august,
under the rock fruit pear,
a limb so stone heavy
it cracks
falling into the dry grass
beside her.

The fat women
across the street
watch from their veranda,
three generations
and a portable barbecue,
corn on the cob and talk
about the fish cannery
not gettin unemployment
to see em through winter.

She pulls the turnips
the pearl potatoes
in her dead husband's garden,
gathering the windfall apples
like money found in the grass
like the red lips
of the kisses he'd promised.

Arnold over the fence
in his tarpaper shack
where they found his father
last spring
dead three days
over a sink of dirty dishes,
the same father who,
after she'd pruned
her apple tree
knocking down one
of his six television antennas,
said the only words
he ever spoke to her,
"put it back up, hippie."

The neighbors smoking salmon
in a <u>Johnny on the Spot</u>
borrowed from the bean fields,
smoke
from the crescent moon vent
curling through beet stalks
so far gone
they are not recognized
as she gathers the seed.

The neighbor lady
watering asparagus,
in the same anklets
and acetate slacks,
the same conversation,
the phone
her husband
a customer
their payments
taking in sewing
the phone.

Arnold
in his ten thousand dollar
black and red pick-up
going to the volunteer firemans'
Wednesday night poker meet,
saying he'd like to break
their neck if anyone parks
on his lawn while he's gone,
and she says she ain't tellin
what woman in town's
in love with his truck,
and he says she's crazy
but she's good lookin.

She watches the sun
behind the bay islands,
watches the fat women
go inside
sitting framed in the windows,
only their laps
only the hinge
of their coffee arm
moving from the saucer
to their lips

— to record this day.